GYMNASTICS

A&D Xtreme
BOLD HI-LO NONFICTION
An imprint of Abdo Publishing
abdobooks.com

ALEX MONNIG

TAKE IT TO THE XTREME!

GET READY FOR AN EXTREME ADVENTURE! THE PAGES OF THIS BOOK WILL TAKE YOU INTO THE THRILLING WORLD OF GYMNASTICS. WHEN YOU HAVE FINISHED READING THIS BOOK, TAKE THE XTREME CHALLENGE ON PAGE 45 ABOUT WHAT YOU'VE LEARNED!

ABDOBOOKS.COM

Published by Abdo Publishing, a division of ABDO, PO Box 398166, Minneapolis, Minnesota 55439. Copyright © 2023 by Abdo Consulting Group, Inc. International copyrights reserved in all countries. No part of this book may be reproduced in any form without written permission from the publisher. A&D Xtreme™ is a trademark and logo of Abdo Publishing.
102022
012023

Design: Series Designer Kelly Doudna, Mighty Media, Inc.
Production: Mighty Media, Inc.
Editor: Liz Salzmann
Cover Photograph: Amy Sanderson/AP Images
Interior Photographs: A.RICARDO/Shutterstock Images, pp. 42–43; AJ MAST/AP Images, pp. 40–41; Amy Sanderson/AP Images, pp. 38–39; AP Images, pp. 6–7, 9, 10–11, 12–13, 16, 17; CRAIG FUJII/AP Images, pp. 28–29; DIETER ENDLICHER/AP Images, p. 27; Doug Pensinger/Getty Images, pp. 30–31; John Gaps/AP Images, pp. 25, 26; JOHN GAPS III/AP Images, p. 32; Juice Dash/Shutterstock Images, p. 44; Keystone Press/Alamy Photo, p. 8; Leonard Zhukovsky/Shutterstock Images, pp. 4–5, 36–37; Michele Morrone/Shutterstock Images, p. 1; Rusty Kennedy/AP Images, pp. 14–15; SANTIAGO LYON/AP Images, p. 24; STEPHANIE MAZE/AP Images, pp. 22–23; SUSAN RAGAN/AP Images, pp. 33, 34–35; Suzanne Vlamis/AP Images, pp. 18–19, 20–21
Design Elements: ayagiz/iStockphoto (hexagon texture); huseyintuncer/iStockphoto (turf); LeArchitecto/iStockphoto (lights); Roman Bykhalets/iStockphoto (dots)

LIBRARY OF CONGRESS CONTROL NUMBER: 2022940528

PUBLISHER'S CATALOGING-IN-PUBLICATION DATA

Names: Monnig, Alex, author.
Title: Gymnastics / by Alex Monnig
Description: Minneapolis, Minnesota : Abdo Publishing, 2023 | Series: Xtreme moments in sports | Includes online resources and index.
Identifiers: ISBN 9781532199301 (lib. bdg.) | ISBN 9781098274504 (ebook)
Subjects: LCSH: Gymnastics--Juvenile literature. | Gymnasts--Juvenile literature. | Sports--History--Juvenile literature.
Classification: DDC 796.44--dc23

TABLE OF CONTENTS

GYMNASTICS BEGINNINGS

Early elements of gymnastics can be traced back to ancient Greece. But modern gymnastics began in the 1800s. That's when German educator Friedrich Jahn invented much of the equipment that's used today. Since then, gymnastics has become a popular sport around the world.

US Olympic gymnast Gabby Douglas
practices on the uneven bars during
the 2016 Olympic Games.

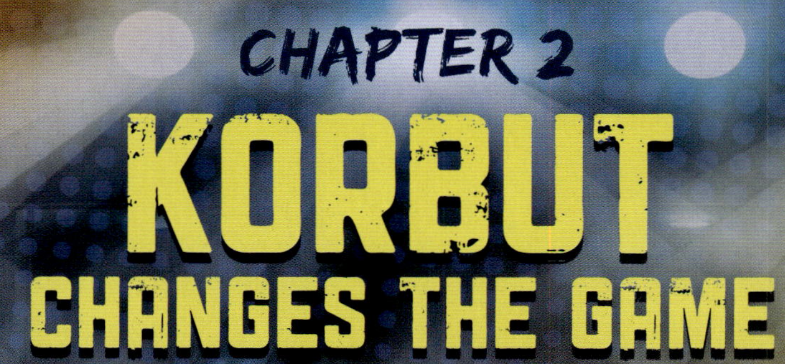

For many years, gymnastics was viewed as an artistic, graceful activity. Then Olga Korbut of the Soviet Union revolutionized the sport. Her athleticism and inventiveness changed gymnastics forever.

Korbut competed at the Olympic
Games in 1972 and 1976.

Korbut won a silver
medal for the uneven
bars at the 1972
Olympic Games.

8

At the 1972 Olympic Games, Korbut introduced exciting new gymnastics moves. One was the first backward somersault on the balance beam. She said that instead of thinking of the beam as a **tightrope**, she tried to think of it as a floor.

XTREME FACT
Korbut's daring routines earned her three gold medals and a silver medal at the 1972 Olympic Games.

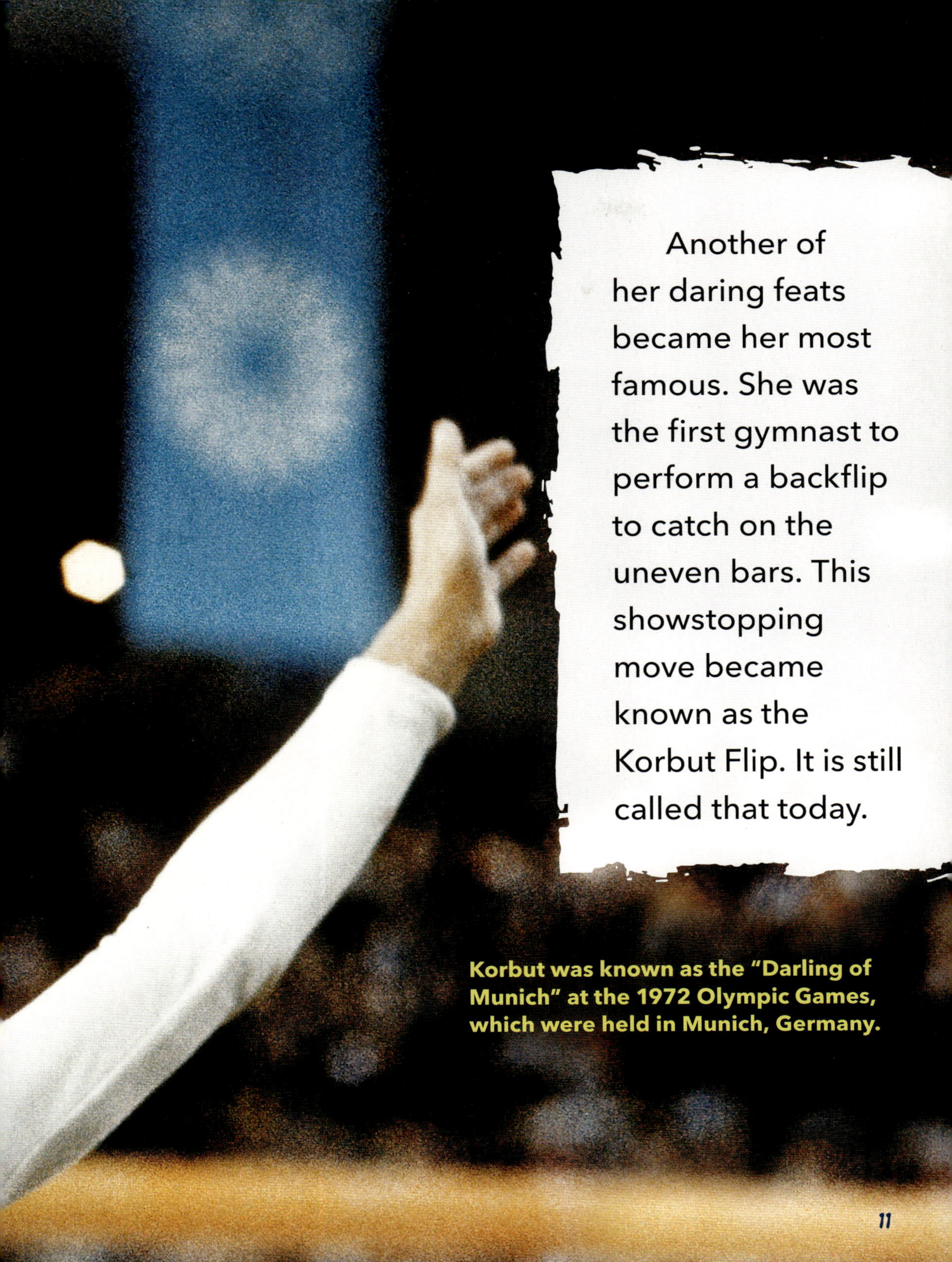

Another of her daring feats became her most famous. She was the first gymnast to perform a backflip to catch on the uneven bars. This showstopping move became known as the Korbut Flip. It is still called that today.

Korbut was known as the "Darling of Munich" at the 1972 Olympic Games, which were held in Munich, Germany.

CHAPTER 3

FUJIMOTO WINS GOLD

Fujimoto's teammate Sawao Kato (*pictured*) also competed in the 1968 and 1972 Olympic Games.

At the 1976 Olympic Games, the Japanese team was expected to win the team **all-around** gold medal. After all, they'd done so at the four previous Olympics. Shun Fujimoto wasn't one of the major stars in the team. By the end of the Games, he would be.

XTREME FACT

Fujimoto's fight through the pain is one of the greatest moments in gymnastics history. When asked years later if he'd do it again, he said he wouldn't. The knee injury ended Fujimoto's competitive career. He went on to become a gymnastics coach.

During an early round of the team floor exercise, Fujimoto **shattered** his kneecap when he landed incorrectly. But Fujimoto didn't want to let his country or his teammates down. So, he kept his injury secret. In spite of the extreme pain of every landing, he continued to compete.

Fujimoto performs on the pommel horse during a 1972 competition.

15

Japan was chasing the Soviet Union for the gold medal. Fujimoto's last event was the rings. At the end, he landed from nearly eight feet (2.4 m) in the air, further injuring his destroyed kneecap. But he scored a personal best 9.7 points. His performance helped Japan win its fifth straight gold medal.

Japan's Mitsuo Tsukahara won the individual gold medal for the horizontal bar at the 1976 Olympic Games.

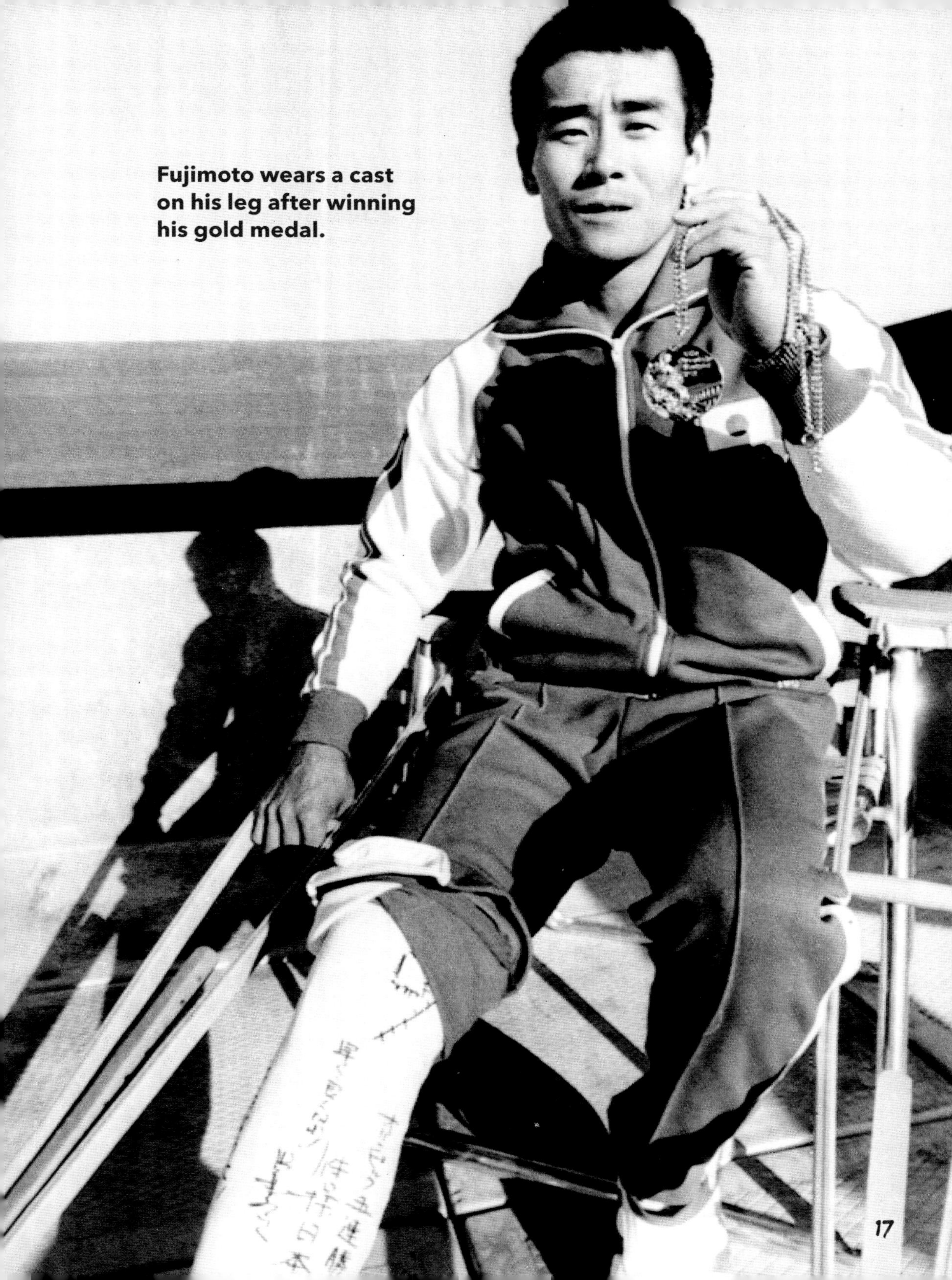

Fujimoto wears a cast on his leg after winning his gold medal.

COMĂNECI'S PERFECT 10

There had been plenty of amazing performances at the Olympics before 1976. But none of them had been perfect in the eyes of the judges. That changed with 14-year-old Nadia Comăneci's uneven bars routine in the team competition.

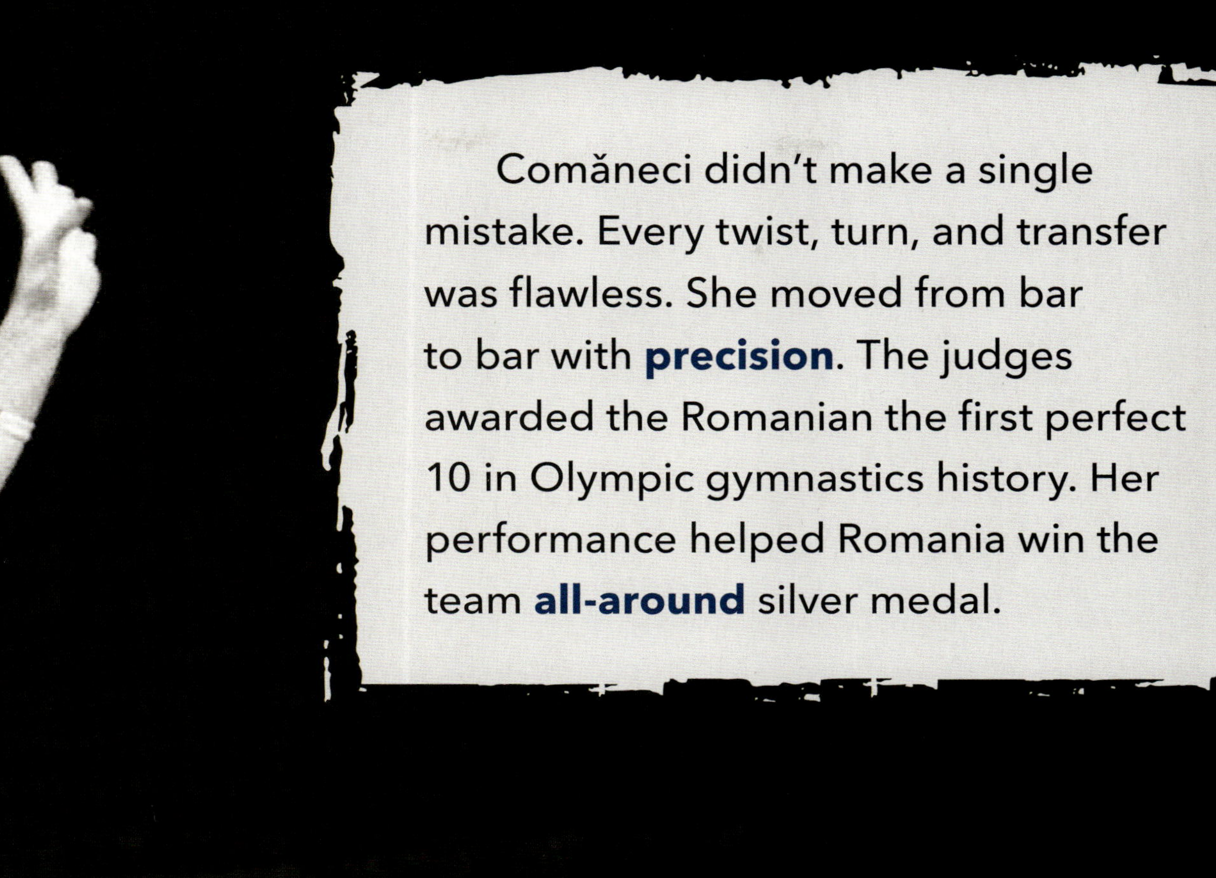

Comăneci didn't make a single mistake. Every twist, turn, and transfer was flawless. She moved from bar to bar with **precision**. The judges awarded the Romanian the first perfect 10 in Olympic gymnastics history. Her performance helped Romania win the team **all-around** silver medal.

Comăneci soars off the uneven bars to land a perfect-10 performance.

SPIETH

A multiple-exposure image shows Comăneci's movements during one of her perfect-10 balance beam routines.

XTREME FACT

In 1976, few people thought scoring a perfect 10 was possible. So, Olympic scoreboards only had enough room for three digits and a **decimal point**. The highest score they could show was 9.99. This meant that Comăneci's perfect 10 was shown as 1.00 on the scoreboard.

The teenager was just getting started. Before the end of the Olympics, Comăneci would receive another six perfect 10s. These included three more on the uneven bars and three on the balance beam. In all, she won three gold medals, a silver medal, and a bronze medal at the 1976 Olympics.

Comăneci performs a flip on the balance beam.

CHAPTER 5
SCHERBO'S SIX GOLDS

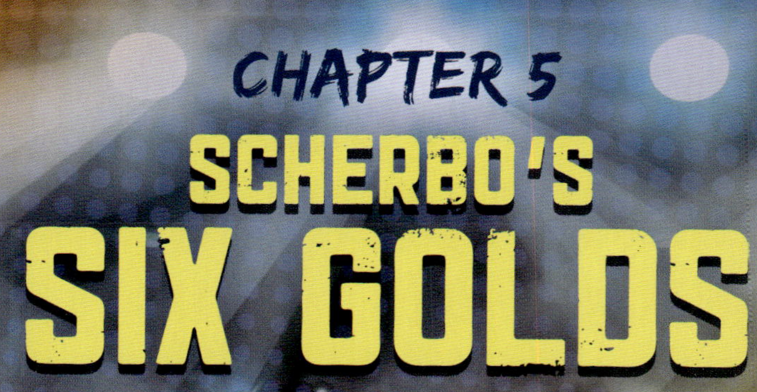

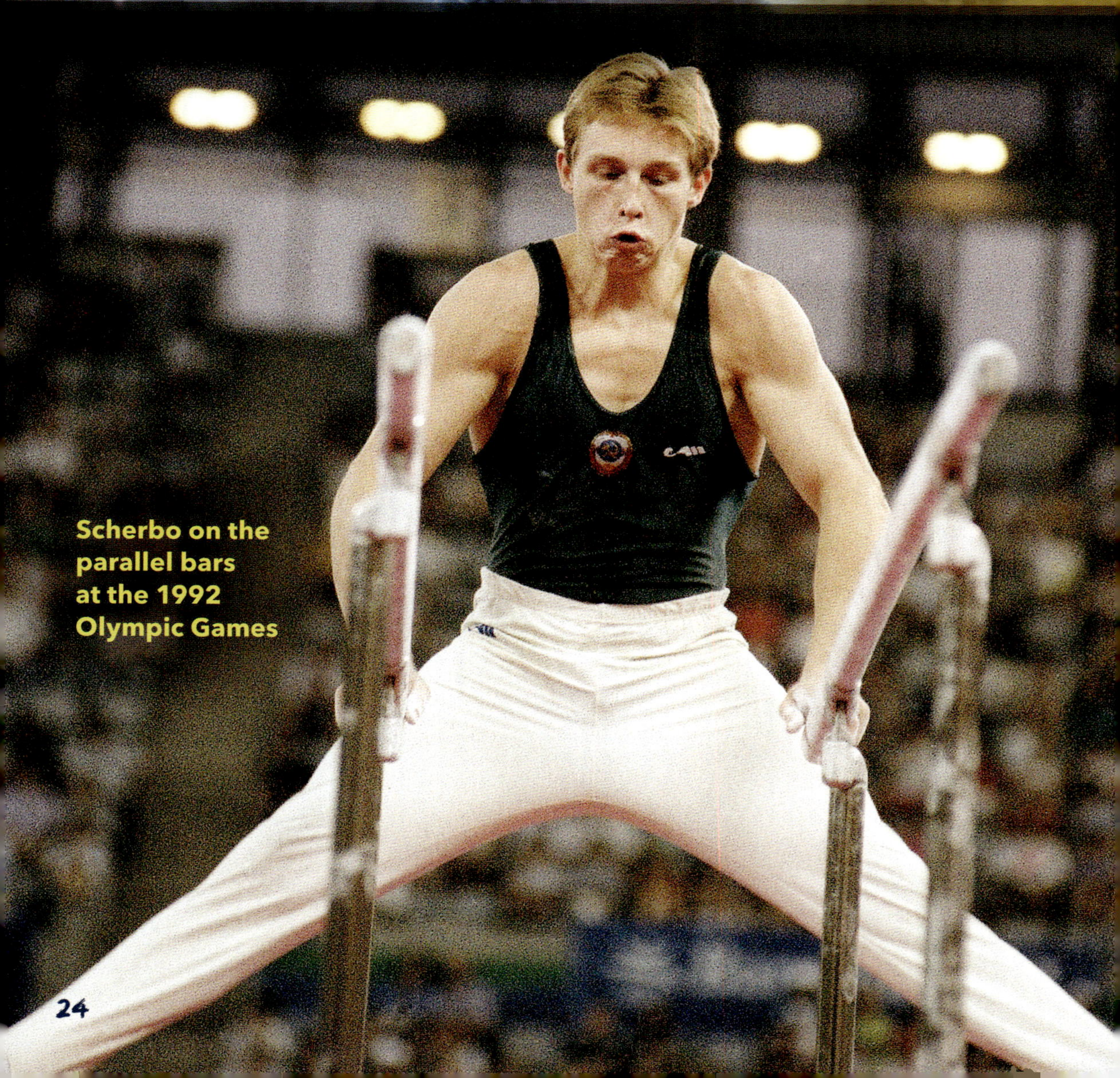

Scherbo on the parallel bars at the 1992 Olympic Games

At the 1992 Olympic Games, Vitaly Scherbo of Belarus competed as part of the **Unified Team**. Over the first few days, Scherbo won both the team and the individual **all-around** gold medals. By the end, he would make Olympic history.

Scherbo (*center*) holds up his individual all-around gold medal.

August 2 was the last day of gymnastics competition. What Scherbo did that day was truly amazing. He won gold in the parallel bars, vault, and rings and tied for gold in the pommel horse. He became the first Olympic athlete to win four gold medals in one day.

Scherbo performs on the rings (*left*) and the pommel horse.

In total, Scherbo won six of the eight gold medals in men's gymnastics. At the time, it was the most gold medals won by a gymnast during a single Olympic Games. Scherbo's performance at the Olympics will forever stand as one of the best in gymnastics history.

Scherbo (*right*) and North Korea's Gil-Su Pae (*center*) tied on the pommel horse. So, they each received a gold medal. Germany's Andreas Wecker (*left*) won the bronze medal.

XTREME FACT

Along with his Olympic success, Scherbo won 23 career World **Championship** medals. That stood as a record until 2019, when Simone Biles won her 24th.

CHAPTER 6

STRUG'S PAINFUL GOLD MEDAL

The US women had never won the team **all-around** Olympic gold medal. At the 1996 Olympics, the team known as the Magnificent Seven was determined to change that. One gymnast, Kerri Strug, would have to fight through extreme pain to make it happen.

Strug performs her
balance beam routine at
the 1996 Olympic Games.

The US had a good lead with just the vault left to go. But then disaster struck. Strug's teammate Dominique Moceanu did poorly on her two vaults. So did Strug on her first try. Even worse, she injured her ankle in an awkward landing.

Strug does a handspring over the vault at the 1996 Olympic Games.

Strug collapses and holds her injured ankle after landing her second vault.

XTREME FACT

Unfortunately, Strug's ankle injury kept her from competing in individual events later in the Olympics. The 1996 team **all-around** would be her only Olympic gold medal.

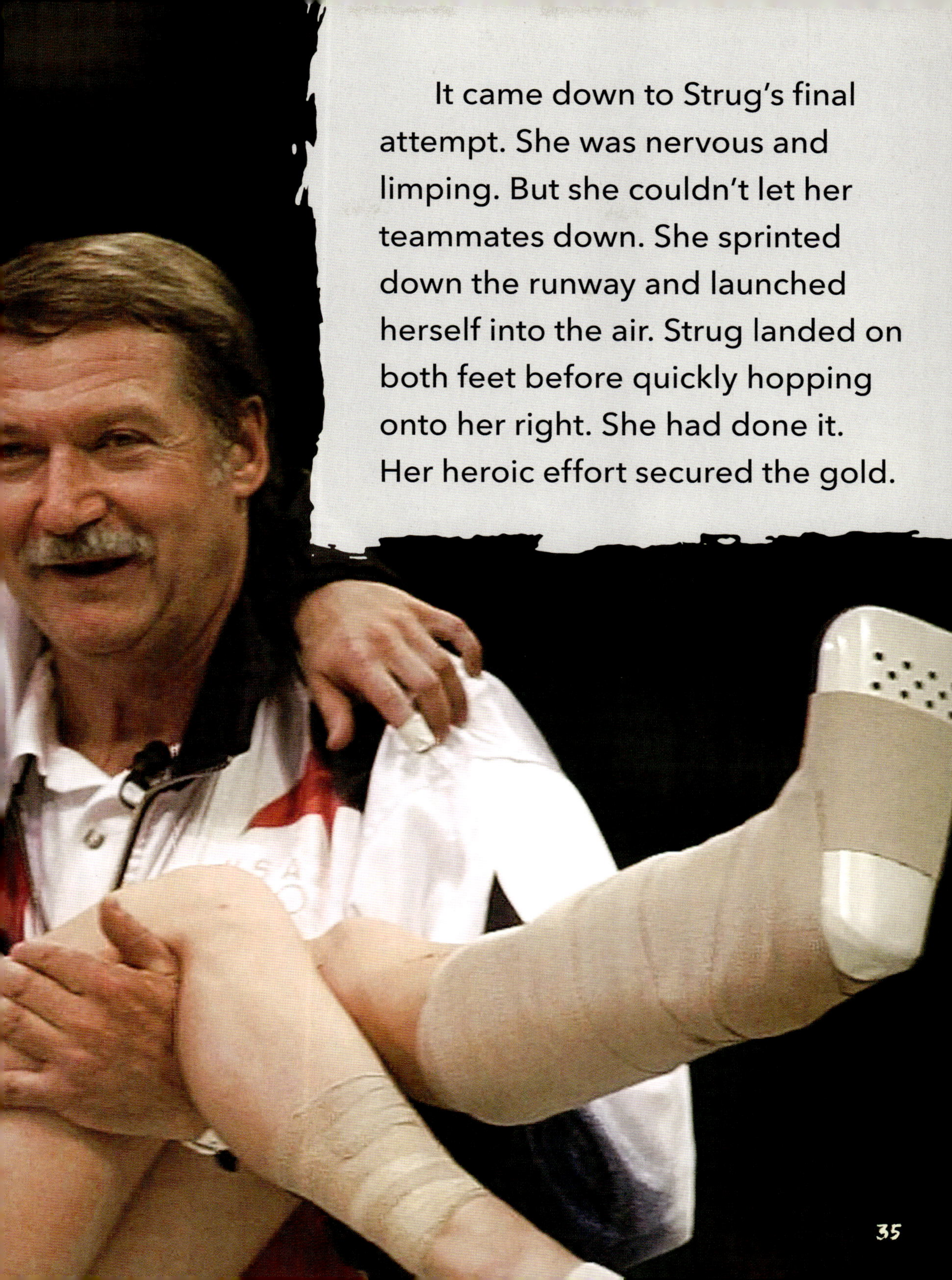

It came down to Strug's final attempt. She was nervous and limping. But she couldn't let her teammates down. She sprinted down the runway and launched herself into the air. Strug landed on both feet before quickly hopping onto her right. She had done it. Her heroic effort secured the gold.

CHAPTER 7

BILES SETS A NEW STANDARD

In 2021, US gymnast Simone Biles was just 24 years old. But many people already consider her to be the greatest gymnast of all time.

At the 2016 Olympic Games, Biles won gold medals in four events, including floor exercise.

Biles is one of just two American gymnasts with seven Olympic medals. She won five at the 2016 Olympic Games. She won two more at the 2020 Olympic Games. And in 2019, she broke the record for most World **Championship** medals.

Biles broke the record for most World Championship medals with a gold medal for the balance beam.

Then at the 2021 US Classic, Biles did something no female gymnast ever had. She completed a Yurchenko double pike vault in competition. She started with a roundoff back handspring onto the vault. Then she did two pike flips before landing on the other side.

Biles clasps the back of her legs during her double pike flip off the vault.

XTREME FACT

From the 2013 US **Championships** to the 2019 World Championships, Biles won every **all-around** competition she entered.

Only men had done this vault routine previously. It was one thing to have the courage to even try it. Having the skill to land it was another. Biles was moving so quickly that she took a few little hops backwards on the landing. But she remained on her feet to make history.

CHAPTER 8

THE FUTURE
OF GYMNASTICS

The courage and skill of amazing athletes from around the world have pushed gymnastics to greater heights. Simone Biles, Sunisa Lee, and Daiki Hashimoto are just a few of the latest superstars to thrill fans and make gymnastics memories.

TAKE THE QUIZ BELOW AND
PUT WHAT YOU'VE LEARNED TO THE TEST!

1) Do you think Shun Fujimoto and Kerri Strug made the right decision to continue competing while injured?

2) On what apparatus did Nadia Comăneci perform her first perfect 10?

3) Would you rather win an Olympic gold medal or invent a new gymnastics move that is named after you? Why?

4) In which event did Vitaly Scherbo tie for gold?

5) Why did Simone Biles withdraw from the 2020 Olympic Games in Tokyo?

GLOSSARY

all-around—the combined scores from all events at a gymnastics competition.

championship—a game, a match, or a race held to find a first-place winner.

decimal point—a dot that separates a whole number from part of a whole number.

precision—the quality or state of being very accurate or exact.

shattered—destroyed or badly damaged.

tightrope—a rope or wire stretched tight that an acrobat performs on.

Unified Team—the name used at the 1992 Summer and Winter Olympic Games for the team of athletes from some of the countries that had been part of the Soviet Union.

ONLINE RESOURCES

To learn more about gymnastics, please visit **abdobooklinks.com** or scan this QR code. These links are routinely monitored and updated to provide the most current information available.

INDEX